NATIONAL ISSUES FORU

The bicentennial of the Bill of Rights provides a particularly timely occasion for reexamining the First Amendment and the civics lesson it was intended to teach. James Madison, Thomas Jefferson, and the others who framed the Bill of Rights were products of the Enlightenment era. Among other things, the First Amendment expressed a characteristic theme of that era by questioning authority. By guaranteeing free speech, the First Amendment guards against the tendency of government to silence individuals who oppose the way official power is used.

Reflecting the emphasis of the Enlightenment era on the power of reason, the First Amendment recognizes the importance of a well-informed public. To the framers of the Bill of Rights, however, the concept of an informed public had a slightly different meaning than the one we attach to that phrase. In the Enlightenment era, being well informed meant having certain factual information — but it also meant thoughtfulness and the exercise of judgment.

Free speech is essential in a democratic nation, the framers of the Bill of Rights were convinced, because reaching public judgment requires considering various perspectives and comparing our views against opposing perspectives. The First Amendment serves as a reminder that a wide range of points of view must be presented in the marketplace of ideas to enable us, as citizens, to reach public judgment.

Those of us who have been involved over the past ten years in the National Issues Forums — a nationwide association of citizens who come together in community forums for nonpartisan discussion about public issues — have taken that lesson to heart. In this issue book, we examine the pros and cons of several points of view on free speech and when and how it should be restricted.

At a time of growing public concern about words and images that are racist, inflammatory, or pornographic, freedom of expression has become a prominent issue on the public agenda. But there is reason for concern about the tone of public discussion about free speech and how communities should respond when confronted with words and images that many people find offensive.

As Donald Downs, a political scientist at the University of Wisconsin, says in a recent book, *The New Politics of Pornography,* "Activists on all sides in the recent debate have often taken emotional and polarizing stands. Neither anti-porn activists nor anti-censorship liberals have shown much willingness to understand their opponents' concerns. There has simply been a clash of views. The extreme positions have demeaned the quality of public discourse on this issue and have jeopardized the quality of democratic debate."

Our purpose in this issue book on freedom of expression — and in public forums on this topic — is not to advocate any single solution or point of view. It is, rather, to encourage constructive debate in which various perspectives are taken seriously. Our goal is to provide a forum in which concerned citizens can discuss this divisive issue, air their differences, think them through, and work toward acceptable solutions.

After the Forums meet each year, the NIF convenes meetings with policymakers to convey the outcome of the discussions. So we can convey participants' thoughts and feelings about this issue, two ballots are included at the end of this book. Before you begin reading these materials, and then again after you have read them and taken part in Forums, I urge you to fill out these ballots and mail them back to us.

This book, like the others in this series, is a guide to one of the nation's pressing issues and an invitation to engage in public discussion and debate about it.

Keith Melville

Keith Melville, Managing Editor

Managing Editor: Keith Melville
Writers: Tom Piazza,
Keith Melville
Research: Bill Carr
Editors: Harris Dienstfrey,
Betty Frecker
Ballots: Amy Richardson,
John Doble, Randa Slim
Production Manager:
George Cavanaugh

Designer: Greg Sundberg Design
Circulation Coordinator:
Victoria Simpson
Cover Illustration: David Gothard
Word Processing: Valerie Breidenbach
Jenifer Williams
Formatting: Parker Advertising
Graphic Research: Bill Carr
Production Director: Robert E. Daley

The books in this series are prepared jointly by the Public Agenda Foundation — a nonprofit, nonpartisan organization devoted to research and education about public issues — and by the Kettering Foundation. They are used by civic and educational organizations interested in addressing public issues.

In particular, they are used in local discussion groups that are part of a nationwide network, the National Issues Forums (NIF). The NIF consists of more than 3,000 civic and educational organizations — colleges and universities, libraries, service clubs, and membership groups. Although each community group is locally controlled, NIF is a collaborative effort. Each year, convenors choose three issues and use common materials — issue books such as this one, and parallel audio and videotape materials.

Groups interested in using the NIF materials and adapting its approach as part of their own program are invited to write or call for further information: National Issues Forums, 100 Commons Road, Dayton, Ohio 45459-2777. Phone 1-800-433-7834.

The NIF issue books — both the standard edition and an abridged version at a lower reading level, as well as audiocassette and videocassette versions of the same material — can be ordered from Kendall/Hunt Publishing Company, 2460 Kerper Boulevard, Dubuque, Iowa 52004-0539. Phone 1-800-338-5578. The following titles are available:

The Boundaries of Free Speech: How Free Is Too Free?
America's Role in the World: New Risks, New Realities
Energy Options: Finding a Solution to the Power Predicament
The Battle over Abortion: Seeking Common Ground in a Divided Nation
Regaining the Competitive Edge: Are We Up to the Job?
Remedies for Racial Inequality: Why Progress Has Stalled, What Should Be Done
The Day Care Dilemma: Who Should Be Responsible for the Children?
The Drug Crisis: Public Strategies for Breaking the Habit
The Environment at Risk: Responding to Growing Dangers
Health Care for the Elderly: Moral Dilemmas, Mortal Choices
Coping with AIDS: The Public Response to the Epidemic
The Public Debt: Breaking the Habit of Deficit Spending

ISBN 0-8403-6924-7

THE BOUNDARIES OF FREE SPEECH: HOW FREE IS TOO FREE?

PREPARED BY THE PUBLIC AGENDA FOUNDATION

CONTENTS

TOXIC TALK: DEFENDING OURSELVES AGAINST OFFENSIVE MESSAGES

"The air and the airwaves are filled with crude language and caustic messages, and there is renewed debate about where to draw the line. When faced with offensive messages, how should communities respond?"

A question for America in the 1990s: Is there anything that cannot be said publicly, and is not being said? Freedom of expression is, once again, a major issue in the United States. Crude language and offensive subjects seem to bombard us from all sides. Movies, television, and the work of many comedians and rock groups have reopened an old debate. Where should we draw the line prohibiting certain kinds of speech? Who should draw it? And should it be drawn at all?

Popular entertainment isn't the only area in which the debate rages. Campuses, too, have been the scene of confrontations. Incidents such as crossburnings and other forms of racial harassment have been on the rise. An increase in ethnic slurs and hate speech has caused many to question what students should be allowed to say under the protection of free speech.

The problem is drawn most clearly in popular culture. A generation ago, comedian Lenny Bruce was arrested for using obscene language in his nightclub act. Today, comedians such as Andrew Dice Clay and others routinely appear on television and radio using language that might have shocked even Lenny Bruce. Some defend even the most tasteless performances by saying that all speech must be protected. The Constitution's First Amendment, which guarantees that freedom, applies to unpleasant expression as well as points of view that many people find repugnant. Others believe that the liberties many performers take threaten America's moral fabric.

Describing this situation, *Time* magazine writer Richard Corliss observes, "There's an acrid tang in nearly every area of American pop culture. Heavy metal masters Motley Crue invoke images of satanism, and the Beastie Boys mime masturbation on stage. . . . Comedians like Sam Kinison and Howard Stern bring locker-room laughs to cable TV and morning radio. On network TV, sitcom moms get snickers with innuendoes about oral sex. In movies, the F-word has become so common, like dirty wallpaper, that the industry's conservative ratings board doesn't even bother to punish the occasional use of it with an R-rating."

The *Miami Herald*'s John Underwood warns that, "In a society where anything goes, everything eventually will." Many are increasingly concerned about revers-

DAVID GOTHARD

ing this tide of offensive expression. Others, however, argue just as strongly that any censorship represents an unacceptable limit to our liberties.

AS NASTY AS THEY WANNA BE

What, exactly, has caused many people to be so upset? The sharpest criticism has been reserved for rock acts that use obscene language and actions to make their points. Things have come a long way since 1957, when Elvis Presley appeared on Ed Sullivan's TV show. Part of Presley's act was his way of shaking his hips suggestively. Concerned about offending viewers, the show's producers told the cameramen to shoot Presley from the waist up. Yet today, HBO is willing to show rock star Madonna faking masturbation onstage.

"Things have gotten out of control," says Joanne Masokowski, founder and director of a California organization called Bay Area Citizens Against Pornography. To illustrate her point, she refers to the lyrics of a 2 Live Crew rap song entitled "S and M." By Masokowski's count, the song contains 117 explicit references to male genitals and 87 references to oral sex. The word "bitch" is used more than 100 times, and "f—" well over 200 times. "There has to be some moderation here," Masokowski says. "It can't keep going in the direction it's been going for the past ten years."

Although 2 Live Crew is one of the most prominent examples, other groups are pumping out songs full of images of sex, violence, and ethnic bias. Take the popular heavy-metal band Guns 'N' Roses for example. In a track entitled, "One in a Million," which begins "Immigrants and faggots, they make no sense to me. . . ." the group spreads a gospel of intolerance and seems to be saying it's OK to hate entire groups of people.

FRANK MICELOTTA/OUTLINE PRESS

Andrew Dice Clay: Pushing the limits in the no-holds-barred 1990s

HATE SPEECH ON CAMPUS

Under the protection of the First Amendment, some very objectionable views are being aired. Many see these instances as part of a larger pattern. They point to a rise in hate speech on college campuses across the country. Blacks, Asians, Jews, and gays have all been targets of racial slurs and even physical harassment.

In the spring of 1988, for example, at Northern Illinois University, white students confronted a black student at a campus bar. As he was leaving the bar, they shouted "Niggers, go home" and "Niggers, we ought to lynch you." In 1991, Brown University expelled a student for shouting abusive statements about Jews, blacks, and gays late at night in a campus courtyard. A student-faculty discipline committee found him guilty of "flagrant disrespect for the well-being of others."

These are hardly isolated examples. Organizations that monitor such incidents agree that there has been an upward trend recently. According to the National Institute Against Prejudice and Violence, bias-motivated incidents occurred on 174 campuses between September 1986 and December 1988. By the end of 1990, the number of campuses on which such incidents were reported had risen to 300.

There is growing support for various measures to fight that trend. More than 100 American colleges and universities have taken steps to restrict offensive forms of expression. In the words of Emory University's director of equal opportunity, "I don't believe freedom of speech on campus was designed to allow people to demean others."

Elsewhere, too, various efforts have been taken to curb offensive speech. In 1990, columnist Jimmy Breslin was temporarily suspended by New York *Newsday* for making racist and sexist remarks to a colleague. Andy Rooney, a commentator on TV's "60 Minutes," was also suspended after supposedly making unflattering remarks about blacks and gays. And the federal government has taken steps to crack down on sexual material in the mails and on the airwaves.

State and city governments have also gotten involved. In October 1990, the director of Cincinnati's Contemporary Arts Center was indicted on charges of displaying obscene photographs. At issue was an exhibition by photographer Robert Mapplethorpe. The show included photos of nude children and of men in overtly sexual poses. And in June of that year, U.S. District Court Judge Jose Gonzalez, in Fort Lauderdale, Florida, banned an album by 2 Live Crew. In a now-famous decision, the judge declared the album to be offensive to the community. In the opening lines of his ruling, he commented that the case was "a battle between two ancient enemies, anything goes and enough already."

RESTRAINING THE CENSORS

For every group that is fighting what they consider to be offensive speech and messages, another is denouncing censorship. Many argue that, as offensive as some of these messages are, censorship is not the way to deal with them.

In the San Francisco Bay area, Bobby Lilly, the chairman of Californians Against Censorship Together, says that record numbers of people have signed the group's petitions against censorship. "There is a division in this country," Lilly says, "over what is moral, proper, and ethical. The question is: How much variation, how much choice, do you allow?"

Two hundred years after the passage of the Bill of Rights, the meaning of the First Amendment is again being hotly debated. Paul Joseph, of the American Civil Liberties Union (ACLU), puts it this way: "We're entering a period of national hysteria over censorship, a time when it is particularly important for people to understand why speech must be allowed, rather than suppressed."

The First Amendment has the brevity and simplicity of a biblical commandment. It says that "Congress shall make no law . . . abridging the freedom of speech, or of the press." Few words in the Constitution are so familiar and few are so important. Yet freedom of speech has never been considered an absolute right. The right to free speech is constantly being balanced against the community's need to maintain order.

In 1919, Supreme Court Justice Oliver Wendell Holmes wrote, "The best test of truth is the power of thought to get itself accepted in the competition of the market." All kinds of thoughts, he said, should be allowed to circulate freely in the marketplace of ideas. But just the same, he argued, there are times when societies that value personal freedom must limit speech. "The most stringent protection of free speech would not protect a man in falsely shouting 'fire' in a theater and causing panic. . . . The question in every case is whether the words used . . . create a clear and present danger that they will bring about substantive evils that Congress has a right to prevent."

FRAMING THE DEBATE

The debate over free speech requires us to balance the right of free expression against the claims of public morality and the general welfare. It poses questions to which people give very different answers. At what point does expression of rebellious or repulsive ideas become a threat to public welfare? Which messages pose a social danger, and why? How can we protect free speech without hurting other things we value, such as diversity and tolerance?

We may not reach agreement on what kinds of messages are too corrosive to be allowed. Still, it is a matter of great importance to ask how communities should respond when confronted with offensive messages. If official censorship is not appropriate, what action is appropriate?

In this discussion, we will examine the pros and cons of three perspectives on free speech and censorship. The first is the argument for the use of government censorship to fight offensive speech. Advocates of this view say that some messages are so destructive that the law must be used to defend against them.

A second perspective argues that the government should not censor speech, but that private institutions can and should. Colleges, radio and television stations, magazine and book publishers all have a right to restrict offensive messages, according to this view.

A third perspective argues for a strict interpretation of the First Amendment. Advocates of this view insist that very few forms of expression pose a clear and present danger to the community. Except for extreme instances, such as hard-core child pornography, those who hold this view argue that even the most offensive expression should not be restricted.

These three positions frame the debate over freedom of expression. Two hundred years after the Bill of Rights was ratified, the meaning of the First Amendment needs to be reexamined. We need to ask how free is too free and which restrictions are too restrictive in a nation committed to individual rights! ■

CHOICE #1
CLEAR AND PRESENT DANGER: THE CASE FOR LEGAL SANCTIONS

"Words and images that are obscene, hatemongering, or an inducement to violence pose a real danger. Strict limits, backed up with the force of law, are warranted when speech poses a threat to our physical and moral well-being."

Jack Thompson, Susan Brownmiller, and Engedaw Berhanu are three people who have very little in common. But each believes that certain messages pose a clear danger. And all three conclude that certain messages should be restricted by law.

Thompson is a Florida attorney who is against obscenity in popular entertainment. He transcribed the lyrics of 2 Live Crew's albums and distributed them to state law enforcement officials. This led to legal action against the rap group for its album *As Nasty as They Wanna Be.*

"This album isn't about free speech," Thompson says. "Its purpose is to titillate and outrage, and glorify the rape of women. These guys are promoting the idea that women are there for nothing but to satisfy men's desires. This stuff makes it more likely that women will be abused."

Susan Brownmiller is the author of *Against Our Will: Men, Women, and Rape*. She was also one of the founders of a New York-based organization called Women Against Pornography. Her chief concern is that violent pornography hurts women.

"I feel surrounded by it," says Brownmiller. "I can't go to the newsstand without being confronted by pictures of women mutilated, tortured, spread into ridiculous postures — pictures designed, I feel, to humiliate my sex and my dignity as a woman."

Engedaw Berhanu is not a well-known figure in Portland, Oregon. But a lawsuit he filed resulted in one of the most prominent recent court cases in that part of the country. Berhanu's nephew, Mulugeta Seraw, was a young Ethiopian living in Oregon and hoping to go to college there. In 1988, he was attacked by three young white skinheads who beat him to death with a baseball bat.

The three young men pleaded guilty to the attack, saying they were adherents of a group called the White Aryan Resistance. The group, based in California, is run by a 53-year-old television repairman named Thomas Metzger, and his son, John. On behalf of Seraw's family, Berhanu brought charges against Metzger's group. Because the organization encourages hatred of blacks and other minorities, the suit said, the group's leaders are responsible for Seraw's death.

SPEECH MATTERS

The common thread in these three individuals' concerns is that speech matters. In this view, words and images shape attitudes, which in turn shape behavior. In the words of Tottie

DAVID GOTHARD

Ellis, vice-president of the Eagle Forum, a conservative, pro-family group, "Words have power in our lives. They make things happen."

When words and images are obscene, pornographic, profane, violent, or hate-mongering, they may cause great harm.

People who share this perspective believe that official measures must be taken to restrict offensive and possibly dangerous messages. These measures, they feel, should include censorship by public agencies such as the Federal Communications Commission and the Justice Department. "Censorship is not the only answer," says Tottie Ellis, "but it is part of the answer. . . . Society has the right to prevent or control that which brings about its own destruction."

Consider the messages that bombard Americans on a typical day. Violence, murder, and adultery are now routinely portrayed on prime-time television programs. In some communities, cable television carries messages from hate groups such as the White Aryan Resistance. Prominent radio personalities specialize in dirty language and ethnic slurs. Magazine stands feature row after row of magazines full of explicit sex.

"To a degree," writes *Time* magazine essayist Charles P. Alexander, "entertainment reflects what's going on in society. But isn't it possible that pop culture reinforces and amplifies bad behavior? Too much of today's entertainment carries messages that are damaging to young psyches and dangerous to society. Among them: 1) women are sexual objects to be used and abused by men; 2) violence is an effective means of resolving conflicts; 3) it is OK to hate another class of people."

Advocates of this first view point to messages conveyed by some of today's most prominent entertainers. Andrew Dice Clay and his offensive references to women are a prime example. Clay's favorite nursery rhyme begins "Peter, Peter, pumpkin eater/ Had a wife, loved to beat her. . . ." and goes downhill from there. Many who hear Clay's routines come away convinced that he is role-modeling all the wrong attitudes — and doing so in sold-out performances.

Clay and other such performers get top billing and make top dollar. Critics feel they are using the protection of the First Amendment to profit from routines that are damaging to society. In a landmark decision, Chief Justice Warren Burger warned against such misuse. "To equate the free and robust exchange of ideas and political debate with commercial exploitation of obscene materials," he wrote, "demeans the grand conception of the First Amendment and its high purpose."

Those who advocate official restrictions point out that government regulates many things that are considered dangerous. When certain chemicals, foods, or drugs are found to be harmful, the government restricts or bans their use. Yet offensive messages — which are just as dangerous, according to those who hold this first view — are given the protection of the First Amendment. Columnist George Will puts it this way: "We legislate against smoking in restaurants. Yet singing 'Me So Horny' [a 2 Live Crew song many find offensive] is a constitutional right. . . . Only a deeply confused society is more concerned about protecting lungs than minds."

Juan Williams, a black reporter for the *Washington Post*, is concerned about 2 Live Crew's impact on the black community. The group, he says, "is selling corruption — self-hate — to vulnerable young minds in a weak black America." Lyrics of such groups distort a healthy conception of "good sex, good relationships, and good times."

While many of those who favor censorship are conservatives, Susan Brownmiller says that liberals should be

RANDY TAYLOR/GAMMA LIAISON

Hatemongers: When speech encourages violence, should it be restricted?

JANETTE BECKMAN/OUTLINE PRESS

2 Live Crew: Mass-marketed filth, or a reflection of a rawer, more culturally diverse reality?

> "Censorship is not the only answer, but it is part of the answer. Those who call for more control understand that society has the right to prevent or control that which brings about its own destruction."
>
> — Tottie Ellis

equally concerned. "Pornography . . . is dangerous, and it incites people to commit violent acts," she says. "The anti-pornography movement must convince people that they can be good liberals, support the First Amendment, have a terrific sex life — and oppose pornography and fight to curtail it."

EVIDENCE OF DANGER

Those who take this perspective are convinced that some messages pose a real danger, and they cite studies that support their views. Some of these studies have indicated that exposure to violent pornography makes men more likely to abuse women.

Research conducted by social psychologist Edward Donnerstein suggests just that. Donnerstein says that men who are exposed to these materials are more likely to believe that they might commit a rape, or that women want to be raped. Such exposure also increases aggressive behavior toward women in a lab setting.

Other researchers have found a link between the increase in rape and the availability of pornography. Police reports often link pornography to the commission of sex crimes. In the words of former Surgeon General C. Everett Koop, "Impressionable men — many of them still adolescents — see this material and get the impression that women like to be hurt, to be humiliated, to be forced to do things that they do not want to do. It is a false and vicious stereotype."

Many are also concerned about the effects of exposure to non-sexual violence. According to the National Coalition on Television Violence, the average American watches eight to ten hours of violent programming each week. "Because of TV," says James Alan Fox, a Northeastern University researcher, "we've become quite used to murder. By repetition, the viewer becomes desensi-

ULTRAVIOLENCE: MAYHEM GOES MAINSTREAM

A few years ago, who would have imagined that one of this season's top-grossing films (Jonathan Demme's *The Silence of the Lambs*) would be about a psychopath who not only murders women but also skins them? Or that meanwhile, over in the world of letters, a young novelist, Bret Easton Ellis, would describe in revolting detail women (and, less notoriously, men, children, and dogs) being tortured and butchered? Or that his novel, *American Psycho*, suppressed by its original publisher, boycotted by feminists, and savaged by critics, would become a best-seller? Or that MTV would still be blaring last year's hit song (Aerosmith's "Janie's Got A Gun") about a teen incest victim pumping a bullet into her daddy's brain?

Arnold Schwarzenegger in *The Terminator*

Sure, ultraviolent fare has always been out there — but up until now, it's always been *out there*, on the fringes of mass culture. Nowadays it's the station-wagon set, bumper to bumper at the local Cinema 1-2-3-4-5, that yearns to be titillated by the latest schlocky horror picture show. And the conglomerated, amalgamated media corporations obligingly churn out increasingly vicious movies, books, and records. Mayhem has gone mainstream.

America's addiction to make-believe violence is like any other addiction: it takes more and more to accomplish less and less. Thirty-two people get offed in *RoboCop* (1987). The 1990 sequel serves up 81 corpses. People are upset by the assault of brutal imagery on radio, TV, in the theaters, in best-selling books. It is not any one film or program that is singularly disturbing, it is the appalling accretion of violent entertainment. It is the sense that things have gotten out of control.

There is legitimate alarm at what all this imaginary violence might be contributing to in an increasingly dangerous real life. According to a *Newsweek* poll conducted by the Gallup organization in March 1991, 40 percent think movie violence is a "very great" cause of the real kind, and an additional 28 percent see it as a "considerable" factor. (Only 11 percent answered "very little.")

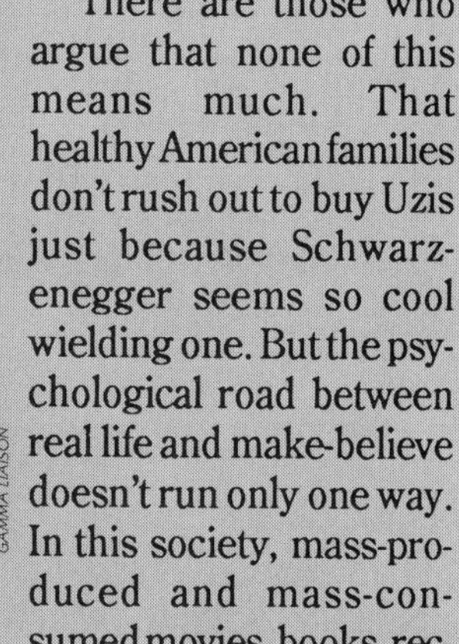

There are those who argue that none of this means much. That healthy American families don't rush out to buy Uzis just because Schwarzenegger seems so cool wielding one. But the psychological road between real life and make-believe doesn't run only one way. In this society, mass-produced and mass-consumed movies, books, records, and TV programs are a considerable part of our real lives; they contribute greatly to making us behave the way we do. To argue otherwise is to consign the arts to a total passivity — always mere reflections, never real influences.

The popular arts are certainly quick enough to claim allegedly positive effects of their noble-farmer movies, triumph-of-the-spirit novels, and anti-drug rock records; they ought to accept some blame for the negative ones. Because we are being so inundated with violent images it is almost impossible to resist growing numb. We risk becoming insensitive to the horror of suffering.

tized to it. It's less of a taboo. In a sense, prime time has unleashed a permit for murder."

Several years ago, University of Illinois psychologists Leonard Eron and L. Rowell Huesmann studied the effects of violent TV shows on children who watch them. They found that 8-year-old children who watched significant amounts of violent programming were more likely to commit crimes as adults. In the investigators' words, "We believe that heavy exposure to televised violence is one of the causes of aggressive behavior, crime, and violence in society."

In different ways, say advocates of this view, both pornography and hatemongering messages are morally harmful and should be restricted. This was the message conveyed by the authors of a minority report of the 1970 Presidential Commission on Obscenity and Pornography: "Society has a legitimate concern in maintaining moral standards. It follows that government has a legitimate interest in attempting to protect such standards against any source which threatens them."

WHAT CAN BE DONE

Official actions of various kinds have been taken to restrict corrosive messages. Advocates of this choice favor a 1988 decision by Kansas City, Missouri, to prevent the Ku Klux Klan from appearing on public access cable TV. The city council voted to close down the public access channel rather than allow the hate group to present its show. (A year later, faced with a lawsuit, the city council reversed its decision.)

In April 1990, the city council of Memphis, Tennessee, signed an ordinance that advocates of this choice applaud. The law bans minors from performances involving "nudity, sexual excitement, sexual conduct, excess violence, or sadomasochistic abuse." Moreover, the law specifies fines for producers and performers who expose minors to such shows, as well as for parents who let their children attend.

Florence Leffler, a Memphis City Council member who voted for the proposal, says she believes offensive lyrics contribute to the deterioration of American society. "I'll do everything I can to try to protect the minds of young people from that kind of garbage," she says.

As of early 1991, no arrests had been made under the new law. But, according to Beth Wade, managing director of the Mid-South Coliseum, some bands now clean up their act when they come to Memphis. Comedian Andrew Dice Clay passed up Memphis entirely on a recent national tour when officials refused to promise that he wouldn't be arrested.

People who hold this view sometimes disagree about what kinds of speech should be restricted. Some are less concerned about offensive lyrics or comedy routines than they are with pornographic magazines. Others worry less about either than about the hate speech of groups like White Aryan Resistance.

What they agree on is that strict limits on freedom of expression — backed up by the force of law — are needed when speech represents a danger to our wellbeing. As important as freedom of speech is, they feel, it is not the only thing we value. As Midge Decter, executive director of the Committee for the Free World, points out, "We have reached a point of extreme confusion in this society. We no longer have any idea what our values are. If the law cannot involve an assertion of community standards, what is it for?"

WHAT CRITICS SAY

Most critics of this position acknowledge that offensive messages exist. But they disagree about the extent of the problem, and they don't feel that legal sanctions are the way to deal with it.

Critics deny that there is a tidal wave of such "verbal sludge." While controversial performers such as Andrew Dice Clay and 2 Live Crew get a lot of attention, their acts are hardly typical. In fact, say some critics, raunchy acts may even reflect important, if unpleasant, aspects of our culture.

The call for censorship, say critics, is also based on a misunderstanding of the problem. Most critics of this position agree that violence is a serious problem in American society. But, according to writer Robert Shea, "The notion that pornography causes sex crime is magical thinking, on a par with the medieval belief that witches cause plagues." Ideas and images certainly influence behavior. But the connection between images, fantasies, and behavior is much more complicated than simple cause-and-effect.

Critics say that, when legislators begin to regard certain words as unacceptable, the results can be absurd. As evi-

MIRKO ILIC

"What the censors are offering is nothing more than the old fantasy of prohibition. Ban racist speech, and no one will be a racist; ban pornography, and no one will ever have a perverse thought again."

— David Rieff

dence, they offer a bill passed by the Colorado House of Representatives in 1991, prohibiting negative comments about fruit, vegetables, and dairy products. A 1989 controversy over a spray used on apples had slowed sales of apples. The bill's supporters wanted to make sure that other farm products would be protected from negative publicity.

To free-speech advocates, this is a revealing example of a serious problem. Once laws are passed prohibiting certain kinds of malicious comments, it seems to make sense to extend the same protection to other areas. Eventually, many messages are prohibited because they are negative, and we are free to say very little.

Another ill effect of official sanctions is that they may intimidate creative people to the point of self-censorship. Over the past few years, the Federal Communications Commission (FCC) has cracked down on radio and TV stations that broadcast offensive material. In the words of attorney Timothy Dyk, "Even if material has serious merit — plays, films, or even dance — it may be found to be indecent. The effect has been self-censorship, because no one wants to be fined by the FCC."

DON WRIGHT/THE PALM BEACH POST

WHY CENSORSHIP DOESN'T WORK

Critics of this position oppose such measures as the Memphis ordinance holding performers responsible for what minors see or hear in live performances. Soon after the ordinance was passed in 1990, the American Civil Liberties Union (ACLU) challenged it. They claimed that the law deprives parents of the right to determine what their children view or don't view.

One of the people involved in that case, a former Air Force sergeant named Larry McDaniel, says: "They're taking away my rights as a parent. That's what ticks me off. These people don't send my kids to school or pay my bills, and yet they turn around and tell my children what concerts they can and cannot go to." Critics of censorship agree. It is the parents' responsibility to monitor what their children see and do.

As critics see it, even hate groups such as the White Aryan Resistance shouldn't be muzzled. They feel that the Kansas City Council was wrong to eliminate its public access channel in order to avoid televising programs produced by the Ku Klux Klan. A lawsuit filed by the ACLU said, in part: "It is easy to support a public forum when the message carried over it is in the mainstream. It is not so easy, for most people, when the message is hateful and wrongheaded. But public access programming is a public forum, the electronic equivalent of a soapbox. It is no different from a public park or street available for political speeches and demonstrations."

Similarly, an Oregon ACLU spokesman said it is wrong to punish the leaders of the White Aryan Resistance on the grounds that their propaganda may have led to the vicious attack that resulted in the death of Mulugeta Seraw. The expression of ideas — however offensive — is protected by the First Amendment. Its main point, say critics, is that all views may be heard. Bad messages may be countered or argued against, but they should not be censored.

As the Supreme Court declared in an important decision, "All ideas having even the slightest redeeming social importance — unorthodox ideas, controversial ideas, even ideas hateful to the prevailing climate of opinion — have the full protection of the guaranties, unless excludable because they encroach on the limited area of more important interests."

Imposing official restrictions is not the best way to deal with offensive speech, conclude critics. In the words of Richard Corliss, "You may despise the work of Clay . . . or 2 Live Crew, and still embrace the concept of an America that allows them to find or lose an audience. They have the right to offend. You have the right to be offended. That is still the American way." ■

CHOICE #2
SELF-IMPOSED RESTRICTIONS: THE PRIVATE-SECTOR SOLUTION

"While government censorship is ill advised, sensible limits should be enforced by private institutions. Publishers, radio and TV stations, college campuses, and other institutions should restrict offensive speech when it violates community standards."

Some people favor public measures as the best way to restrict offensive messages. But others who are equally concerned about corrosive speech favor a different remedy. They feel that government should not prevent potentially offensive messages from being heard. But, they say, private institutions such as radio and TV stations, publishers, and concert producers, should exercise judgment about what they will broadcast or publish.

A series of recent incidents suggests that executives in many private firms have begun doing just that. Book publishers, TV stations, and others have drawn the line when faced with words or images that are tasteless or offensive.

In 1990, for example, TV commentator Andy Rooney was temporarily removed from his post on "60 Minutes" after he was quoted as saying that blacks have "watered down their genes because the less intelligent ones . . . have the most children" — a remark Rooney denies having made. David Burke, then president of the CBS News Division, issued a stern announcement: "CBS News cannot tolerate such remarks, or anything that approximates such comments, since they in no way reflect the views of this organization."

Top-40 radio stations acted similarly in 1987 when pop singer George Michael released his recording "I Want Your Sex." Station managers were concerned that the song condoned casual sex at a time when AIDS and other sexual diseases were rampant. Many decided not to air the record, and they were widely praised for their decision. MTV returned the video of "I Want Your Sex" to Columbia Records with a complaint about "unacceptable visuals."

In November 1990, MTV drew the line about another video it considered offensive, Madonna's "Justify My Love." Madonna says the video illustrates her erotic fantasies. MTV said it was too hot to handle. Simon and Schuster, one of America's largest publishers, made a similar decision in 1990. The publisher decided not to publish a book for which it had paid $300,000 to author Bret Easton Ellis. The book was *American Psycho*, which graphically depicts the murder and dismemberment of men, women, children, and animals.

FRANK MICELOTTA/OUTLINE PRESS

Madonna controversy: "Justify My Love," said MTV, was too hot to handle.

INDUSTRY STANDARDS

Advocates of private-sector restrictions agree that America is suffering from a deluge of offensive messages. But the private-sector solution doesn't put the authority of the law behind rules about what can be said in public. The best way to reflect community standards, in this view, is to let private institutions decide what is acceptable.

Private companies have a right and a duty to determine which messages are consistent with their corporate responsibility and the audiences they serve, and to define limits to the kinds of speech they will permit.

"No society can survive if the only rule is 'anything goes,'" writes essayist

Charles Alexander. "So the question becomes, 'What goes?' In general, this question should be answered not by government but by artists, producers, theater owners, and media executives."

Those who agree with this perspective point to the way the entertainment industry changed its message about drugs in the 1980s. In the 1960s and 1970s, drug use was often portrayed as glamorous and socially acceptable. Rock groups used drug imagery openly, and movies such as *Easy Rider* glorified it. But in the 1980s, as the use of hard drugs rose, the entertainment industry voluntarily began changing the signals it sent. This has played a large role, many feel, in changing Americans' attitudes toward drugs.

Advocates of this second choice say it is wrong to assume that every serious problem requires government action. They feel that censorship (along with other official restrictions) is too blunt a tool with which to handle fine distinctions regarding freedom of speech.

That was Louisiana Governor Buddy Roemer's reason for vetoing a 1990 record-labeling bill. The Louisiana bill would have required warning labels on recordings about such matters as deviant sex, violence, bigotry, and drug abuse. It would also have banned the sale of such recordings to minors.

At the press conference where he announced his veto, the governor said he agreed that parents needed to be told about the contents of recordings. But he said that passing a law wasn't the best way to deal with the problem. "In a free America," Roemer said, "where speech is constitutionally protected, the best method of informing the public is through voluntary compliance with industry standards, similar to what the movie industry has done successfully."

CAMPUS CODES

Recently, speech codes have been instituted on more than 125 American campuses. They are the clearest example of the measures private institutions are taking to limit offensive messages. The codes, which were rare until a few years ago, are a response to a rash of demeaning comments and actions directed against women and minorities. Incidents of bias-motivated harassment have been reported on many campuses. In 1990, People for the American Way, a nonprofit group based in Washington, D.C., made a study of the problem. Of the 128 institutions of higher learning they surveyed, 60 percent reported such incidents over the previous 18 months. Fifty-seven percent of the institutions said that intolerance is a significant problem.

Some examples: at the University of Michigan, flyers were distributed in 1987 calling for an "open season" on blacks, and referring to them by insulting names. Soon after, the campus radio station broadcast racially offensive jokes. In October 1990, a Dartmouth College student weekly, the *Dartmouth Review*, published anti-Semitic passages from Hitler's autobiography, *Mein Kampf.* On other campuses there have been reports of Native American, gay, and female students being publicly humiliated.

Whether the issue is racist, sexist, or anti-gay messages on campus, advocates of speech codes insist that harassment must be taken seriously. To protect and promote diversity, they say, rules must be clearly spelled out about what kinds of speech will not be tolerated.

DAVID GOTHARD

SEXIST HARASSMENT

Sexist harassment of women is one of the key themes in the troubling pattern of intolerance on campus. Sexist harassment ranges from sexual innuendo or inappropriate comments — often in the guise of humor — to verbal harassment, inappropriate touching, subtle pressure for sexual activity, and coerced sexual relations.

A typical example of such sexist harassment is a practice called "scoping," in which college men publicly describe and rate women's attractiveness. On several campuses, college men regularly sit at tables next to the cafeteria line. As women go through the line, the men loudly assess their attributes and hold up rating signs ranging from one to ten. In several instances, there are reports that women have chosen to avoid the embarrassment of running this offensive gauntlet either by skipping meals or finding other places to eat.

No reliable survey exists to gauge the extent of sexist harassment on campuses nationwide. But surveys taken on several campuses suggest that the problem is widespread. A 1986 survey at Cornell University, for example, found that 78 percent of the women students had experienced sexist comments and 68 percent had received unwelcome attention from their male peers — most often individuals rather than group harassment. In another survey taken at the University of Rhode Island, 70 percent of the women said they had been insulted by men's sexist remarks.

"Peer harassment sends the message that a woman is not being taken seriously as a person," write Jean O'Gorman Hughes and Bernice Sandler in a report entitled *Peer Harassment: Hassles for Women on Campus*, which is distributed by the Association of American Colleges. "When men harass with impunity, the implication is that women are fair game and that such harassment is acceptable behavior. Just as institutions should prevent and deal with instances of racial harassment, they should also prevent and deal with instances of peer harassment based on sex."

REASONS FOR HARSH MEASURES

Advocates of speech codes say that racist insults don't deserve First Amendment protection. Such insults are intended not as ideas to be considered, but as blows. Like blows, they are not meant to encourage dialogue.

Charles Lawrence, law professor at Stanford University, says, "The experience of being called 'nigger,' 'spic,' 'Jap,' or 'kike' is like receiving a slap in the face. Racial epithets and harassment often cause deep emotional scarring, and feelings of anxiety and fear that pervade every aspect of a victim's life."

More than 100 universities have adopted speech codes to restrict offensive speech. The punishments for breaking the rules range from written warnings to mandatory counseling to expulsion. In the words of Thomasiana Clemons, of the University of Connecticut, "We're trying to discourage people from browbeating others who simply may be different. Racists shouldn't be able to abuse minorities."

On many campuses, students are issued guides explaining what is considered offensive speech or verbal harassment. At the University of Michigan, examples of prohibited behavior include making jokes about gays, displaying a Confederate flag on the door of your room, and making disparaging remarks about women in class. At some private colleges, the standards are even stricter.

Stanford University is one such college. Canetta Ivey, a Stanford student, defends the school's strict codes. "We don't put as many restrictions on freedom of speech as we should," she says. "What we are proposing is not completely in line with the First Amendment. I'm not sure if it should be. We at Stanford are trying to set a different standard from what society at large is trying to accomplish."

WHAT CRITICS SAY

Critics of this approach divide into two camps. Some feel that private-sector restrictions will not be enough to stem the tide of offensive messages. These people feel that only the force of law will be effective. Others are concerned that private-sector restrictions amount to censorship in a different guise. These people feel that either restriction will have damaging effects on free speech.

Those who feel the private-sector solution is inadequate say that the entertainment industry can't really police itself. The profits involved in putting out the best-selling offensive materials are too great. Asking media executives to voluntarily turn their backs on huge profits is not realistic, they say. The reason laws exist is to force people to do the right thing. Therefore, restrictions on offensive speech should be made law.

Others have a different perspective on the private-sector solution. They don't want to see private firms, such as TV stations, apply their own sanctions more often. That would lead, they fear, to speakers and performers censoring themselves.

"Most critics recognize the problems caused by hate speech on campus. But they feel that speech codes are no solution."

Critics note that the incident involving Andy Rooney and "60 Minutes" seems to have done just that. Several months after he returned to the program, Rooney was preparing commentary dealing with the United Negro College Fund. As he prepared it, he found himself cutting out certain comments that he thought would be too sensitive. Finally, the segment was canceled. "I decided it was so touchy I'd better not do it," Rooney says. "In view of my problems, I decided not to push it."

From this perspective, Rooney's problems are our problems. We need public discussion about sensitive subjects such as race, gender, and nationality. If journalists, commentators, and private citizens shy away from these subjects, critics feel, we will all suffer.

Critics of private-sector sanctions are especially concerned about campus speech codes. Most critics recognize the problems caused by hate speech in America's colleges and universities. But they feel that speech codes are the wrong way to handle them.

DON WRIGHT/THE PALM BEACH POST

"For colleges not to deal with racial prejudice on campus is an abdication of their responsibility in a free society," acknowledges Ira Glasser, executive director of the American Civil Liberties Union. "They've got to address these things, but not this way, both because it doesn't work and because it's incompatible with freedom of speech."

Critics point to the University of Michigan's speech code, which they feel is too vague to be helpful. The code bars "ver-

PARENTAL ADVISORY: THE LABELING CONTROVERSY

On September 19, 1985, spokespersons for a newly formed group called the Parents' Music Resource Center (PMRC) appeared before the Senate Committee on Commerce, Science, and Transportation. They wanted to focus public attention on the explosion of raunch in popular music. The group was led by Tipper Gore, the wife of Senator Albert Gore, Jr. of Tennessee.

Because offensive lyrics can have a damaging effect on minors, says Tipper Gore, they should be restricted. The PMRC's goal, however, is not official censorship. They want, instead, to persuade the record industry to voluntarily place stickers on recordings with offensive lyrics. These stickers would warn parents that the recordings might offend some listeners.

The Recording Industry Association of America (RIAA) agreed in 1985 to label some records, cassettes, and compact discs. The RIAA is a recording industry trade group whose members produce 90 percent of the musical recordings released in the United States. The RIAA's decision was made, in large part, as a response to the PMRC's concerns.

Some state legislatures have taken those concerns a step farther. Certain states have begun debating bills that would make warning stickers mandatory, not just voluntary. Most musicians and executives in the recording industry fear that such laws would have a chilling effect on artists. *New York Times* columnist Tom Wicker asks, "Won't some artists be influenced to alter their creative works to avoid labeling and the resulting damage to sales? And if a state can ban, or require retailers to label a commercial recording, why can't it require booksellers to label books, since many contain words or ideas as explicit as any rap lyric?"

To head off legislative measures and mandatory labeling, the RIAA announced a new voluntary labeling policy in March 1990. The association said that record producers would place a uniform, easily recognizable sticker on offensive recordings. The label reads: "Explicit Lyrics—Parental Advisory." The RIAA contends that the new policy is the best way to inform consumers about the abrasive content of some recordings while respecting the First Amendment rights of musicians."

—Bill Carr

bal slurs" based on race, ethnicity, religion, sexual orientation, sex, creed, national origin, ancestry, age, and handicap. It also prohibits "unwelcome sexual advances." These terms are so broad, critics say, that they are likely to lead only to arguments over what constitutes a violation.

Finally, critics are worried about a tendency to judge messages mainly in terms of their potential to offend. That may lead to a situation, says writer David Rieff, in which "all interactions — and for that matter, all institutions — are going to be judged on the basis of their contributions to people's sense of psychological well-being."

As critics see it, there are four reasons why speech codes are the wrong response to offensive speech. Each of these reasons, they say, points up a weakness of most private-sector solutions to this problem:

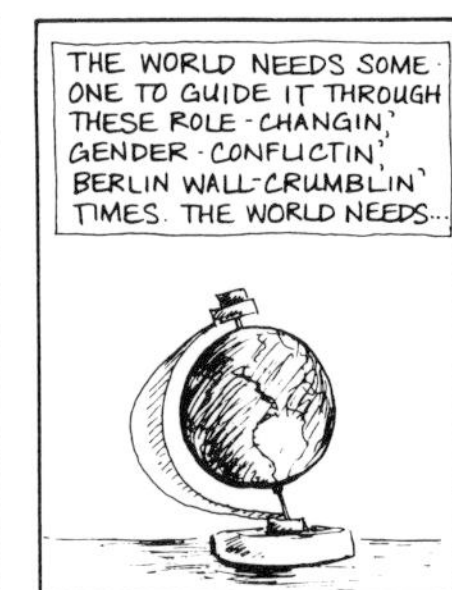

© JEFF SHESOL

Political correctness: New enlightenment on campus or a new form of McCarthyism?

- By driving such speech underground, we miss its message. That makes it harder to combat the attitudes underlying it.
- Since campus speech codes are vague, they tend to be unevenly enforced. This can make their use uneven and unfair.
- Open-mindedness and freedom of expression should be the highest values on campus, but speech codes undercut both of them.
- Codes focus on the symptoms rather than on the causes of prejudice and insensitivity.

Professor Nadine Strossen of New York University Law School says that offensive speech, while ugly, can raise "public consciousness about our society's endemic racism. By driving clear expression of racism underground, we make it harder to combat the attitudes it expresses."

The vagueness of the codes, some say, will result in broader restrictions than were intended. "When you pass a rule that represses speech," says the ACLU's Ira Glasser, "you're passing a rule whose sweep is going to be broader than the things you're trying to contain."

Critics say that some codes leave almost nothing out. The University of Connecticut was recently forced to rewrite a code that prohibited "inappropriately directed laughter, inconsiderate jokes, and conspicuous exclusion of students from conversations." Former Governor Huey Long of Louisiana once said that if fascism came to America it would be in the guise of anti-fascism. Critics say that speech codes prove his point.

Opponents say that speech codes constrict freedom of thought in the places where it should be most important — colleges and universities. "The dominant principle of a university," says Benno C. Schmidt, president of Yale University, "must be freedom of thought. We cannot censor or suppress speech, no matter how obnoxious its content, without violating the principle that is our justification for existence."

Finally, critics say, the real problems are racism and sexism. Imposing codes based only on an idea of what is politically correct is not the way to prevent the spread of hatred and bias.

In the words of Leonard Steinhorn and Louise Arkel, authors of People for the American Way's report on campus ethnoviolence, "Many schools avoid searching for the cause of the problem and instead turn to quick-fix solutions. Too many schools abdicate their most basic role — to educate, to teach students to think critically and challenge easy answers and assumptions. Restricting free speech may contribute to an atmosphere of intolerance, and to an impression that some rights can be short-circuited to protect others." ■

CHOICE #3
FIRST PRINCIPLES AND FREE EXPRESSION: MORE SPEECH, NOT ENFORCED SILENCE

"Because speaking freely is the cornerstone of our liberties, freedom of expression should be abridged rarely, if at all. The best remedy for offensive messages is not restrictions but more speech."

Many Americans are troubled by a sense that anything goes, that nothing is sacred, and that a tide of offensive messages poses an increasing threat. In response, there is growing support for restrictions on offensive speech. These restrictions seem, to many, to be the only way to stem this tide.

But advocates of a third perspective disagree. They believe that freedom of expression should be restricted only in rare instances, if at all. Advocates of this third perspective say there is more harm in restricting speech than in the objectionable speech itself. As Justice Benjamin Cardozo asserted, "Freedom of speech is the indispensable condition of nearly every other form of freedom."

The ten amendments in the Bill of Rights were designed to restrict the role and authority of the government. Advocates of this choice point out that the very first of its amendments specifies that "Congress shall make no law . . . abridging the freedom of speech."

One of our distinguishing features as a nation, say people who take this position, is a strong defense of individual freedom. And that begins with the freedom to think and say what we please, without fear of censorship. In this view, it hardly matters whether restrictions on speech are official, or the result of private-sector action.

TYRANNY OF THE MAJORITY

Not only may Congress "make no law abridging the freedom of speech," say advocates of this third view, it must also preserve that freedom against those who would abridge it.

Some have argued that censorship might be all right if a majority supported it. But advocates of this third view disagree strongly. In the words of Aryeh Neier, former head of the American Civil Liberties Union, "You could suppress

DAVID GOTHARD

virtually anything if all you had to do was submit it to a vote. Our Constitution says that 'Congress shall make no law abridging the freedom of speech.' That is, the democratic process shall not prohibit any speech or expression."

Above all, say civil libertarians, the First Amendment is a tool for protecting minority views against the tyranny of the majority. Minority views, even when they are offensive — or more accurately, *especially* when they are offensive — deserve to be protected. That is why entertainers with offensive messages should not be censored, according to those who advocate this view. As writer Martha Frankel says, "Those of us concerned about First Amendment issues must defend 2 Live Crew's right to make music. But we don't have to pretend that what they have to offer is more than vile drivel with a backbeat."

With the exception of child pornography, where minors are exploited against their will, there is no justification for permitting government to decide what we can see or hear. Above all, from this point of view, no individual or government official should be permitted to be the arbiter of taste or public morality. "The price we pay for freedom of expression," says Danny Goldberg, a manager of rock acts and chairman of the ACLU Foundation in southern California, "is that some things will be considered vile by some people." But, say advocates of this choice, it is a small price to pay to be free to say what we please.

BENNO FRIEDMAN/OUTLINE PRESS

Andy Rooney: Removed from his "60 Minutes" post because of offensive remarks.

WHY FREE SPEECH MATTERS

To advocates of this point of view, a strict defense of free speech makes sense for several reasons. One of them is the encouragement of creativity. In countries where the government curbs freedom of speech, artists are considered instruments of state policy. If their messages don't echo the party line, they are often regarded as dangerous voices that must be silenced.

Advocates of this position say that the creativity of Americans in many areas is the result of a cultural environment in which a wide range of expression is allowed to flourish. In the words of Joe Saltzman, faculty member at the School of Journalism at the University of California, Los Angeles, "Artists . . . should be able to shock their audiences into new areas of thinking or feeling." In fact, many feel that these kinds of expression are the true test of freedom. "The right to free speech is always tested at the extremes," says Aryeh Neier.

Those who feel this way are concerned about any action that silences writers for their point of view. An example is the decision of CBS executives to suspend Andy Rooney of "60 Minutes," for his remarks about gays and blacks. Howard Kurtz, of the *Washington Post,* commented that Rooney's remarks "may be insensitive, muddled, or just plain wrongheaded. But denouncing writers and shutting off the debate will not make the problems go away. If journalism becomes increasingly allergic to controversy, increasingly wary of telling people uncomfortable truths, that will simply create a vacuum to be filled with rumor, whispers, and prejudice."

MARK LEIA LOHA/MEGAFORCE RECORDS

Robb Flynn of heavy metal band Vio-lence: If you don't like the message, say civil libertarians, you can turn away from it or speak out against it.

The same logic, say free-speech advocates, extends to campus speech codes. They believe that efforts to outlaw ugly or insensitive remarks will endanger the right to express other ideas. The commitment to free speech, they say, reminds communities that they must deal with uncomfortable social and political situations.

They point out that the First Amendment was meant to benefit listeners as well as speakers. The right to listen to wide-ranging debate is every bit as important as the right to speak one's mind. If we are to make up our own minds, we have a need to hear competing viewpoints.

"If ideas are too important to suppress, they are also too important to ignore. The whole point of free speech is not to make ideas exempt from criticism but to expose them to it."

—Garry Wills

JUDGING FOR OURSELVES

From this perspective, few forms of speech — neither pornography nor violence in films and television, nor offensive rap or rock lyrics, nor the ravings of the White Aryan Resistance — pose a real danger to us as individuals or as a society. The idea that words cause psychic injury leads to the mistaken conclusion, in editor Lewis Lapham's phrase, that we should "place speech and symbolic gesture in the same category of objects as the tire iron, the nightstick, and the truncheon."

The impulse to censor, say those who agree with this third option, also reflects a lack of faith in the ability of individuals to judge for themselves. The First Amendment rests on what constitutional scholar Archibald Cox refers to as "faith in the ultimate good sense and decency of free people."

As the American Library Association put it in a statement on the freedom to read, "We are deeply concerned about attempts at suppression. Most such attempts rest on a denial of the fundamental premise of democracy: that the ordinary citizen, by exercising critical judgment, will accept the good and reject the bad. The censors, public and private, assume that they should determine what is good and what is bad for their fellow citizens. We trust Americans to recognize propaganda, and to reject it. We do not believe they need the help of censors to assist them in this task."

Every time speech is restricted, say advocates of this choice, our freedom to control our own lives is jeopardized. As feminist attorney Wendy Kaminer puts it: "We cannot look to the government to rid us of pornography. Legislative or judicial control of pornography is simply not possible without breaking down the legal principles and procedures that are essential to our own right to speak and, ultimately, our freedom to control our own lives."

Certain forms of speech cannot be restricted without threatening the principle of free speech itself, advocates of this third view feel. "Censorship," says free-speech lawyer Floyd Abrams, "is contagious. Censorship is habit-forming."

Many civil libertarians fear that censorship poses a serious threat to our freedom. They point to recent Federal Communications Commission restrictions on material to be broadcast. The FCC has a policy of punishing any radio station that airs "patently offensive language" — a term that critics feel is dangerously vague.

As Monroe Price, dean of the Yeshiva University Law School, says, "the threat to broadcasting licenses worth tens and hundreds of millions of dollars — and the prospect of federal prosecution — will have its intended chilling effect." Free-speech advocates fear that chill could extend to any divisive political issue, and that the quality of public debate will drop.

Once censorship starts, say civil libertarians, it is often taken to an extreme. In 1987, for example, a Florida school superintendent, concerned about unhealthy reading material, banned 64 books and plays from his district's schools. Among the works were Shakespeare's *Twelfth Night* and *The Merchant of Venice*, Ernest Hemingway's *The Old Man and the Sea*, F. Scott Fitzgerald's *The Great Gatsby*, and other classics.

Advocates of this choice acknowledge that censorship is nothing new. But experts say that attempts to censor school materials have been on the rise since the early

DAVID GOTHARD

1980s. Some communities have even banned an award-winning version of *Little Red Riding Hood* on the grounds that grandmother had a glass of wine after escaping the wolf.

JUST SAY NO

When we confront offensive messages, what can we do to express our disapproval? One thing we can do, say advocates of this view, is turn away. Most offensive messages, they say, can be ignored. If you find certain TV programs offensive, change the channel or turn off the TV. If magazines in a local newsstand offend you, don't buy them. Some civil libertarians support laws to prevent what is called "thrusting." Thrusting is displaying offensive pictures, speech, or other wares in a way that violates the privacy of passersby. An example is the open display of pornographic magazines at newsstands.

Advocates of the third choice also say that parents should listen to the lyrics on the records their children bring home. If parents find them offensive, they should talk to their children about what is wrong with the messages.

In other words, freedom of speech imposes a responsibility to speak out against what you find offensive. "If ideas are too important to suppress," says political writer Garry Wills, "they are also too important to ignore. The whole point of free speech is not to make ideas exempt from criticism but to expose them to it."

This approach can have a strong effect. Advocates of this option note that Andrew Dice Clay's popularity began to wane because of just such action. Singer Sinead O'Connor refused to appear on the same segment of "Saturday Night Live" as Clay, as did cast member Nora Dunn. Dunn called Clay's words "degrading and repulsive." Bret Ellis's ultraviolent novel *American Psycho* provoked a storm of protest from people who worked at Simon & Schuster, the book's original publisher. Simon & Schuster eventually canceled the book.

Ku Klux Klan demonstration in Houston: Advocating free speech for groups like the KKK may encourage their hateful message.

From this perspective, the best way for universities to deal with racist and sexist attitudes is not to suppress talk about the issues but to get to the root of the problem by encouraging open discussion. On a growing number of campuses, students are required to attend workshops or take classes dealing with questions of race and gender.

WHAT CRITICS SAY

Critics strongly disagree with the idea that the First Amendment was intended to protect virtually all speech. They point out that the Supreme Court has consistently held that obscenity is not protected expression any more than libel or slander are.

They also argue that much of the offensive material protected under the banner of "artistic freedom" is not really art at all. Columnist George Will says, "Corporations sell civil pollution for profit. Liberals rationalize it as virtuous tolerance in 'the marketplace of ideas.'"

The appropriate response to the worst of these messages, say critics, is not tolerance but outrage. To do nothing about such messages because their bad effects can't be proven is a mistake. As *Washington Post* columnist Nicholas von Hoffman notes, many liberals worry about ethnic stereotypes in school textbooks. But, at the same time, they insist that the movies children watch have no effect on them. "Textbooks in every public school in the nation have been overhauled in the last 20 years," he writes, "because it was thought that the blond, blue-eyed suburban children once depicted therein taught little people a dangerous ethnocentrism. If textbooks . . . can have such sweeping effect, what are we to surmise about the effects on the impressionable young of an R- or X-rated movie, in wide-screen technicolor, with Dolby sound and every device of cinematic realism?"

Critics of this third position think that the protection of all speech, no matter how offensive or potentially dangerous, represents individualism taken to an unhealthy extreme. They feel individual rights must be balanced against responsibility to the community. The swelling tide of offensive messages has a coarsening and destructive effect on community life. And that, they say, is why certain restrictions must be imposed.■

GRAPPLING WITH LIMITS: THE LAST WORD ON THE FIRST AMENDMENT

"People disagree about the harm caused by offensive messages and how communities should respond. The question is what we are prepared to tolerate as the price of maintaining our freedoms."

Two hundred years after the Bill of Rights was added to the Constitution, Americans are reexamining the meaning of free speech. The discussion about where to draw the line between what is acceptable and what is not is hardly abstract. In many communities, and on hundreds of campuses, people are trying to define that line, and trying to decide what to do when it is crossed.

Advocates of legal restrictions on offensive speech want existing obscenity laws to be strictly enforced. They would also like to see new laws enacted to stem the tide of "toxic" messages. They approve of Judge Gonzalez's decision to declare 2 Live Crew's album obscene. Extreme instances of free speech must be curbed, they feel, to make community life more wholesome.

Others share these concerns but feel that the private sector, not the government, should deal with them. They believe that musical groups, club owners, and recording executives should police themselves to cut down on offensive material.

Advocates of a strict interpretation of the First Amendment disagree. Even if 2 Live Crew's lyrics are offensive, they feel, the group still has a right to produce them. And people who find the group's message offensive have the right to voice their objections to it. In this view, limitations on anyone's right to free speech threaten everyone's right.

As we have seen, the same array of responses is being debated with regard to a wide range of offensive speech, including racist epithets, raunch radio, and Robert Mapplethorpe's photographs of men in sadomasochistic poses.

DAVID GOTHARD

DAVID GOTHARD

CLASHING VALUES

What are the underlying issues in the debate over freedom of expression? In one respect, the question is how we should regard numerous recent instances of offensive words and images. Are they evidence of a society that has lost its moral compass in which everything is permitted and nothing is forbidden? Or are they indications of a healthy respect for free expression and our willingness to pay the price free expression exacts, which is to tolerate messages that are offensive and uncomfortable?

In another respect, this is a debate about how we resolve the tension between contending values. While free speech is important, it is just one of the things we value. Writing about efforts to restrict pornography, Charles Krauthammer comments that the debate about what should be done amounts to a clash over two fundamental values, individual liberty and public morality. Those who favor censorship, says Krauthammer, "are prepared to admit that restrictions curtail liberty, though a kind of liberty they do not think is particularly worth having. On the other hand, civil libertarians admit that a price of liberty is that it stands to be misused, and that pornography may be one of those misuses. Public morality may suffer, but freedom is more precious. Both sides agree, however, that one cannot have everything and may sometimes have to trade one political good for another."

The debate over free speech is also about the damage caused by offensive words and images. Should they be considered acts of psychological violence — in James Underwood's words, "sordid in-influences that are every bit as harmful as a blow to the head"? Clearly, speech sometimes hurts and those who are offended or injured by it are often inclined to remove the pain by removing the speech. But if measures are taken to restrict speech that causes discomfort, a great many restrictions would have to be put in place and the right to speak freely might be seriously eroded.

There are also differences about the damage done to individual rights whenever certain kinds of speech are restricted. Those who favor additional restrictions — whether campus speech codes, self-censorship in the recording industry, or laws such as the Memphis ban on public performances involving nudity, sexual conduct, and excess violence — feel that such measures can be taken without endangering constitutional rights.

For their part, civil libertarians warn that once certain forms of expression are restricted or banned, would-be censors are likely to find other messages that deserve to be censored. If we begin by banning racial epithets on the grounds that they amount to verbal harassment and then move on (as the Colorado legislature has done) to pass a bill prohibiting disparaging comments about perishable fruit, other such measures are likely to follow — and talking freely will soon be a thing of the past. Perhaps, as Floyd Abrams said, censorship *is* contagious.

If the passionate debate over free speech is a sign of the energizing value of the First Amendment, the divisiveness of the discussion should also be a warning. In an open marketplace of ideas and arguments, disputes are inevitable and even desirable. Yet at times, the debate over free speech threatens to become a shouting match.

At the center of today's debate about free speech is a question that the framers of the Constitution and the Bill of Rights grappled with 200 years ago: What is a proper and acceptable balance between individual rights and the community's need to maintain order and protect itself from threats to its health and safety? How these conflicting objectives are balanced depends on what we value most, and what we are prepared to tolerate as the price of maintaining our freedoms.■

FOR FURTHER READING

For historical perspective on the First Amendment, see the American Civil Liberties Union's briefing paper, *Freedom of Expression*, which traces its roots to the Enlightenment era and describes its role in America's constitutional system (New York: The American Civil Liberties Union, 1991).

For reports that reflect growing concern about tasteless, offensive, or socially corrosive messages, see two recent cover stories in *Time* and *Newsweek*: an article by Richard Corliss entitled "X-Rated" that appeared in the May 7, 1990 issue of *Time* magazine, and an article entitled "Violence in Our Culture," which appeared in *Newsweek*, April 1, 1991.

Attorney Donna Demac takes a comprehensive look at what she regards as the growing threat posed by censors in *Liberty Denied: The Current Rise of Censorship in America* (New York: Pen Center, 1988). *Censorship News*, a newsletter published by the New York-based National Coalition Against Censorship, tracks efforts to restrict freedom of expression.

The National Coalition Against Pornography has produced two reports on the evidence of harm; see "Pornography's Relationship to Rape and Aggression Toward Women," and "Consequences of Pornography Consumption" (Cincinnati: National Coalition Against Pornography, 1990). Sociologist Thelma McCormack reviews the evidence on pornography and comes to quite a different conclusion in "Making Sense of Research on Pornography," a report distributed by the National Coalition Against Censorship.

For thoughtful analyses of pornography and the issues it poses, see Linda Williams's *Hard Core: Power, Pleasure, and the "Frenzy of the Visible"* (Berkeley and Los Angeles: University of California Press, 1989); and Donald Alexander Downs's *The New Politics of Pornography* (Chicago: University of Chicago Press, 1989), which examines the Minneapolis and Indianapolis ordinances, and explores the challenge they pose to free speech.

For accounts of hate speech on campus, see *Hate in the Ivory Tower* (Washington, D.C.: People for the American Way, March 1990), which provides a survey of the wave of intolerance on college campuses and the response to it, and *Campus Ethnoviolence and the Policy Options* (Baltimore: National Institute Against Prejudice and Violence, 1990), a report written by Howard Ehrlich.

For different perspectives on the campus response to hate speech, see Mary Ellen Gale's essay on "Curbing Racial Speech," in the Winter 1990/1991 issue of *The Responsive Community*, an article by Steve French entitled "Hate Goes to College," which appeared in the July 1990 issue of the *ABA Journal*, and "Taking Offense," an article on "political correctness" on campus and the threat it poses to free speech, which appeared in *Newsweek*, December 24, 1990.

ROB SAUNDERS

In "The Campus: 'An Island of Repression in a Sea of Freedom,'" which appeared in the September, 1989 issue of *Commentary*, Chester E. Finn, Jr. expresses concern about campus codes, arguing that such actions threaten the fundamental principle of open debate.

Mari Matsuda, law professor at Stanford University, is the author of an influential article, "Public Response to Racist Speech: Considering the Victim's Story," which appeared in the *Michigan Law Review* (August, 1989). Matsuda calls for universities to forbid hate speech directed at minorities, on the grounds that freedom of speech was intended to protect the powerless.

For two contrasting perspectives on racist speech, see Charles Lawrence's "If He Hollers Let Him Go: Regulating Racist Speech On Campus," which argues in favor of speech codes; and Nadine Strossen's response, "Regulating Racist Speech On Campus: A Modest Proposal?" which warns against the censoring effects of such codes. Both articles appear in the *Duke Law Journal*, Volume 1990, number 3.

ACKNOWLEDGMENTS

We would like to express our appreciation to the people who helped choose this year's topics and took part in discussions about how they should be approached. Once again, David Mathews and Daniel Yankelovich provided both support and guidance. Our colleagues John Doble, Jean Johnson, Jon Rye Kinghorn, Robert Kingston, Suzanne Morse, Patrick Scully, Jeffrey Tuchman, and Deborah Wadsworth played a valuable role in refining the framework and clarifying the presentation.

Finally, our thanks to Loren Siegel at the American Civil Liberties Union and to Howard J. Ehrlich and Robert D. Purvis of the National Institute Against Prejudice and Violence, who provided advice and assistance as we prepared the manuscript.

NATIONAL ISSUES FORUMS

The National Issues Forums (NIF) program consists of locally initiated Forums and study circles which bring citizens together in communities throughout the nation for nonpartisan discussions about public issues. In these Forums, the traditional town meeting concept is re-created. Each fall and winter, three issues of particular concern are addressed in these groups. The results are then shared with policymakers.

More than 1,700 civic and education organizations — high schools and colleges, libraries, service organizations, religious groups, and other types of groups — convene Forums and study circles in their communities as part of the National Issues Forums. Each participating organization assumes ownership of the program, adapting the NIF approach and materials to its own mission and to the needs of the local community. In this sense, there is no one type of NIF program. There are many varieties, all locally directed and financed.

Here are answers to some of the most frequently asked questions about the National Issues Forums:

WHAT HAPPENS IN FORUMS?

The goal of Forums and study circles is to stimulate and sustain a certain kind of conversation — a genuinely useful conversation that moves beyond the bounds of partisan politics and the airing of grievances to mutually acceptable responses to common problems. Distinctively, Forums invite discussion about each of several choices, along with their cost and the main arguments for and against them. Forum moderators encourage participants to examine their values and preferences — as individuals and as community members — and apply them to specific issues.

CAN I PARTICIPATE IF I'M NOT WELL INFORMED ABOUT THE ISSUE?

To discuss public issues, citizens need to grasp the underlying problem or dilemma, and they should understand certain basic facts and trends. But it isn't necessary to know a great deal about an issue. NIF discussions focus on what public actions should be taken. That's a matter of judgment that requires collective deliberation. The most important thing to ponder and discuss is the kernel of convictions on which each alternative is based. The task of the National Issues Forums is not to help participants acquire a detailed knowledge of the issue but to help people sort out conflicting principles and preferences, to find out where they agree and disagree and work toward common understandings.

ISN'T ONE PERSON'S OPINION AS GOOD AS ANOTHER'S?

Public judgment differs from personal opinion. It arises when people sort out their values and work through hard choices. Public judgment reflects people's views once they have an opportunity to confront an issue seriously, consider the arguments for and against various positions, and come to terms with the consequences of their beliefs.

ARE FORUM PARTICIPANTS EXPECTED TO AGREE UPON A COURSE OF ACTION?

A fundamental challenge in a democratic nation is sustaining a consensus about a broad direction of public action without ignoring or denying the diversity of individual preferences. Forums do not attempt to achieve complete agreement. Rather, their goal is to help people see which interests are shareable and which are not. A Forum moderator once described the common ground in these words: "Here are five statements that were made in our community Forum. Not everyone agreed with all of them. But there is nothing in them that we couldn't agree with."

WHAT'S THE POINT OF ONE MORE BULL SESSION?

Making choices is hard work. It requires something more than talking about public issues. "Talking about" is what we do every day. We talk about the weather, or our friends, or the government. But the "choice work" that takes place in Forum discussions involves weighing alternatives and considering the consequences of various courses of action. It means accepting certain choices even if they aren't entirely consistent with what we want, and even if the cost is higher than we imagined. Forum participants learn how to work through issues together. That means using talk to discover, not just to persuade or advocate.

DO THE FORUMS LEAD TO POLITICAL ACTION?

Neither local convenors nor the National Issues Forums as a whole advocate partisan positions or specific solutions. The Forums' purpose is to influence the political process in a more fundamental way. Before elected officials decide upon specific proposals, they need to know what kinds of initiatives the public favors. As President Carter once said, "Government cannot set goals and it cannot define our vision." The purpose of the Forums is to provide an occasion for people to decide what broad direction public action should take.

PRE-FORUM BALLOT

THE BOUNDARIES OF FREE SPEECH: HOW FREE IS TOO FREE?

One of the reasons people participate in the National Issues Forums is that they want leaders to know how they feel about the issues. So that we can present your thoughts and feelings about this issue, we'd like you to fill out this ballot before you attend Forum meetings (or before you read this book if you buy it elsewhere) and a second ballot after the Forum. Before answering any of the questions, make up a three-digit number and fill it in the box at the top of the right margin.

The moderator of your local Forum will ask you to hand in this ballot at the end of the session. If you cannot attend the meeting, send the completed ballot to National Issues Forums, 100 Commons Road, Dayton, Ohio 45459-2777.

Fill in your three-digit number ☐

1. Please indicate whether, over the last ten years or so, the following has increased, stayed about the same, or decreased.

	Increased	Stayed the Same	Decreased	Not Sure
a. The amount of violent material on TV	☐	☐	☐	☐
b. The amount of sexually explicit material on TV	☐	☐	☐	☐
c. The amount of intolerant (e.g., racist, sexist, anti-gay or anti-Semitic) expression	☐	☐	☐	☐

2. How much effect do you think today's violent movies have in causing real violence?

	Check One
a. Considerable	☐
b. Little	☐
c. Not sure	☐

3. The following questions are about pornography — books, movies, magazines, and photographs that show or describe sex activities. Please indicate if you think sexual materials do or do not have that effect.

	Do Have	Do Not Have	Not Sure
a. Sexual materials provide an outlet for bottled-up impulses.	☐	☐	☐
b. Sexual materials lead people to commit rape.	☐	☐	☐
c. Sexual materials lead to the breakdown of morals.	☐	☐	☐
d. Sexual materials provide information about sex.	☐	☐	☐

4. For each of the following forms of speech or expression indicate whether you think it should be: (1) officially banned by the government, (2) privately restricted (relying on the judgment of radio and TV stations, publishers, newsstand owners, college and university administrators, etc.) but *not* restricted by the government, or (3) not restricted by the government or private organizations but left up to the individual's judgment.

	Officially Banned	Privately Restricted	Not Restricted
a. Groups like the Ku Klux Klan have their own cable TV show	☐	☐	☐
b. Songs with unusually violent or sexually explicit lyrics sold in record stores	☐	☐	☐
c. Comedians like Andrew Dice Clay whose material is sexually explicit or racially offensive appearing on TV	☐	☐	☐
d. Students shouting racist remarks on a college campus	☐	☐	☐
e. Male students engaging in sexist harassment or shouting obscenities on a college campus	☐	☐	☐

5. Which of these statements comes closest to your feelings about laws on unusually violent, sexually explicit, or intolerant (racist, sexist) language?

	Check One
a. The government should officially restrict unusually violent, sexually explicit, or intolerant expression. OR	☐
b. Such expression should be privately restricted, (relying on the judgment of radio and TV stations, publishers and newsstand owners, colleges and universities, etc.) but *not* by the government. OR	☐
c. Unusually violent, sexually explicit, or intolerant expression should not be restricted, but individuals should be free to voice their moral disapproval of such expression. OR	☐
d. Not sure	☐

6. Here are some arguments for and against **Choice #1 Clear and Present Danger: The Case for Legal Sanctions.** Whether you like that choice or not, please indicate whether you strongly agree, somewhat agree, somewhat disagree, or strongly disagree with each argument.

	Strongly Agree	Somewhat Agree	Somewhat Disagree	Strongly Disagree	Not Sure
a. Laws must be used to defend against offensive messages.	☐	☐	☐	☐	☐
b. One problem with imposing legal sanctions against offensive speech is that once certain messages are banned, there is no limit where the censorship would stop.	☐	☐	☐	☐	☐
c. Our reluctance so far to prohibit offensive messages has put at risk many of our cherished values.	☐	☐	☐	☐	☐

(next page)

7. Here are some arguments for and against **Choice #2 Self-Imposed Restrictions: The Private-Sector Solution.** Whether you like that choice or not, please indicate whether you strongly agree, somewhat agree, somewhat disagree, or strongly disagree with each argument.

	Strongly Agree	Somewhat Agree	Somewhat Disagree	Strongly Disagree	Not Sure
a. One way to protect community standards is by allowing private institutions to decide on a case-by-case basis what speech or behavior violates local standards.	☐	☐	☐	☐	☐
b. Imposing speech codes on campuses will not combat the underlying problem of prejudice and insensitivity to others' beliefs.	☐	☐	☐	☐	☐
c. Leaving the task of restricting offensive speech to industries such as the media is a guarantee that more offensive messages will be permitted.	☐	☐	☐	☐	☐

8. Here are some arguments for and against **Choice #3 First Principles and Free Expression: More Speech, Not Enforced Silence.** Whether you like that choice or not, please indicate whether you strongly agree, somewhat agree, somewhat disagree, or strongly disagree with each argument.

	Strongly Agree	Somewhat Agree	Somewhat Disagree	Strongly Disagree	Not Sure
a. Restrictions on free speech, whether by official means or by private-sector action, threaten our commitment as a society to protect minority views.	☐	☐	☐	☐	☐
b. Instead of censoring their expression, a better way to deal with racist attitudes on campuses is to encourage open discussion about racial differences.	☐	☐	☐	☐	☐
c. One of the problems with unlimited free speech is that it carries individual rights to such an extreme that responsibilities to the community are neglected.	☐	☐	☐	☐	☐

9. Into which of the following age groups do you fall?

- **a.** 18 to 29 ☐
- **b.** 30 to 39 ☐
- **c.** 40 to 49 ☐
- **d.** 50 to 64 ☐
- **e.** 65 and over ☐

10. Are you white, black, Hispanic, Asian?

- **a.** White ☐
- **b.** Black or African-American ☐
- **c.** Latino or Hispanic-American ☐
- **d.** Asian-American ☐
- **e.** Other ☐

11. What was the last grade of school you completed?

- **a.** Grade school or less ☐
- **b.** Some high school ☐
- **c.** High school graduate ☐
- **d.** Vocational/technical ☐
- **e.** Some college/2 yr. college ☐
- **f.** Four-year college graduate ☐
- **g.** Postgraduate work ☐

12. Are you a male or female?

- **a.** Male ☐
- **b.** Female ☐

13. What is your ZIP CODE? ____________

POST-FORUM BALLOT

THE BOUNDARIES OF FREE SPEECH: HOW FREE IS TOO FREE?

One of the reasons people participate in the National Issues Forums is that they want leaders to know how they feel about the issues. So that we can present your thoughts and feelings about this issue, we'd like you to fill out this ballot after the Forum. Before answering any of the questions, fill in your three-digit number at the top of the right margin.

The moderator of your local Forum will ask you to hand in this ballot at the end of the session. If you cannot attend the meeting, send the completed ballot to National Issues Forums, 100 Commons Road, Dayton, Ohio 45459-2777.

Fill in your three-digit number ☐

---

1. Please indicate whether, over the last ten years or so, the following has increased, stayed about the same, or decreased.

	Increased	Stayed the Same	Decreased	Not Sure
a. The amount of violent material on TV	☐	☐	☐	☐
b. The amount of sexually explicit material on TV	☐	☐	☐	☐
c. The amount of intolerant (e.g., racist, sexist, anti-gay or anti-Semitic) expression	☐	☐	☐	☐

---

2. How much effect do you think today's violent movies have in causing real violence?

	Check One
a. Considerable	☐
b. Little	☐
c. Not sure	☐

---

3. The following questions are about pornography — books, movies, magazines, and photographs that show or describe sex activities. Please indicate if you think sexual materials do or do not have that effect.

	Do Have	Do Not Have	Not Sure
a. Sexual materials provide an outlet for bottled-up impulses.	☐	☐	☐
b. Sexual materials lead people to commit rape.	☐	☐	☐
c. Sexual materials lead to the breakdown of morals.	☐	☐	☐
d. Sexual materials provide information about sex.	☐	☐	☐

---

4. For each of the following forms of speech or expression indicate whether you think it should be: (1) officially banned by the government, (2) privately restricted (relying on the judgment of radio and TV stations, publishers, newsstand owners, college and university administrators, etc.) but *not* restricted by the government, or (3) not restricted by the government or private organizations but left up to the individual's judgment.

	Officially Banned	Privately Restricted	Not Restricted
a. Groups like the Ku Klux Klan have their own cable TV show	☐	☐	☐
b. Songs with unusually violent or sexually explicit lyrics sold in record stores	☐	☐	☐
c. Comedians like Andrew Dice Clay whose material is sexually explicit or racially offensive appearing on TV	☐	☐	☐
d. Students shouting racist remarks on a college campus	☐	☐	☐
e. Male student engaging in sexist harassment or shouting obscenities on a college campus	☐	☐	☐

5. Which of these statements comes closest to your feelings about laws on unusually violent, sexually explicit, or intolerant (racist, sexist) language?

	Check One
a. The government should officially restrict unusually violent, sexually explicit, or intolerant expression. OR	☐
b. Such expression should be privately restricted, (relying on the judgment of radio and TV stations, publishers and newsstand owners, colleges and universities, etc.), but *not* by the government. OR	☐
c. Unusually violent, sexually explicit, or intolerant expression should not be restricted, but individuals should be free to voice their moral disapproval of such expression. OR	☐
d. Not sure	☐

6. Here are some arguments for and against **Choice #1 Clear and Present Danger: The Case for Legal Sanctions.** Whether you like that choice or not, please indicate whether you strongly agree, somewhat agree, somewhat disagree, or strongly disagree with each argument.

	Strongly Agree	Somewhat Agree	Somewhat Disagree	Strongly Disagree	Not Sure
a. Laws must be used to defend against offensive messages.	☐	☐	☐	☐	☐
b. One problem with imposing legal sanctions against offensive speech is that once certain messages are banned, there is no limit where the censorship would stop.	☐	☐	☐	☐	☐
c. Our reluctance so far to prohibit offensive messages has put at risk many of our cherished values.	☐	☐	☐	☐	☐

(next page)

7. Here are some arguments for and against **Choice #2 Self-Imposed Restrictions: The Private-Sector Solution.** Whether you like that choice or not, please indicate whether you strongly agree, somewhat agree, somewhat disagree, or strongly disagree with each argument.

	Strongly Agree	Somewhat Agree	Somewhat Disagree	Strongly Disagree	Not Sure
a. One way to protect community standards is by allowing private institutions to decide on a case-by-case basis what speech or behavior violates local standards.	☐	☐	☐	☐	☐
b. Imposing speech codes on campuses will not combat the underlying problem of prejudice and insensitivity to others' beliefs.	☐	☐	☐	☐	☐
c. Leaving the task of restricting offensive speech to industries such as the media is a guarantee that more offensive messages will be permitted.	☐	☐	☐	☐	☐

8. Here are some arguments for and against **Choice #3 First Principles and Free Expression: More Speech, Not Enforced Silence.** Whether you like that choice or not, please indicate whether you strongly agree, somewhat agree, somewhat disagree, or strongly disagree with each argument.

	Strongly Agree	Somewhat Agree	Somewhat Disagree	Strongly Disagree	Not Sure
a. Restrictions on free speech, whether by official means or by private-sector action, threaten our commitment as a society to protect minority views.	☐	☐	☐	☐	☐
b. Instead of censoring their expression, a better way to deal with racist attitudes on campuses is to encourage open discussion about racial differences.	☐	☐	☐	☐	☐
c. One of the problems with unlimited free speech is that it carries individual rights to such an extreme that responsibilities to the community are neglected.	☐	☐	☐	☐	☐

9. Into which of the following age groups do you fall?

- **a.** 18 to 29 ☐
- **b.** 30 to 39 ☐
- **c.** 40 to 49 ☐
- **d.** 50 to 64 ☐
- **e.** 65 and over ☐

10. Are you white, black, Hispanic, Asian?

- **a.** White ☐
- **b.** Black or African-American ☐
- **c.** Latino or Hispanic-American ☐
- **d.** Asian-American ☐
- **e.** Other ☐

11. What was the last grade of school you completed?

- **a.** Grade school or less ☐
- **b.** Some high school ☐
- **c.** High school graduate ☐
- **d.** Vocational/technical ☐
- **e.** Some college/2 yr. college ☐
- **f.** Four-year college graduate ☐
- **g.** Postgraduate work ☐

12. Are you a male or female?

- **a.** Male ☐
- **b.** Female ☐

13. What is your ZIP CODE? ___________